Elizabeth Park
A Century of Beauty

Written by Alicia Cornelio

Photographs by William Shepard

The Donning Company Publishers
184 Business Park Drive, Suite 206
Virginia Beach, Virginia 23462

    Steve Mull, General Manager
    Barbara Buchanan, Office Manager
    Susan Adams, Project Research Coordinator
    Faye Underwood, Editor
    Andrea L. W. Eisenberger, Graphic Designer
    Mary Ellen Wheeler, Proofreader/Editorial Assistant
    Stephanie Danko, Imaging Artist
    Scott Rule, Director of Marketing
    Travis Gallup, Marketing Coordinator

    Mary Taylor, Project Director

Library of Congress Cataloging-in-Publication Data

Cornelio, Alicia.
      Elizabeth Park : a century of beauty / written by Alicia Cornelio ; photographs by William Shepard.
          p. cm.
  Includes bibliographical references (p.).
      ISBN 1-57864-241-8 (hard cover : alk. paper)—ISBN 1-57864-242-6 (soft cover : alk. paper)
  1. Elizabeth Park (Hartford, Conn.) 2. Elizabeth Park (Hartford, Conn.)—Pictorial works. 3. Hartford (Conn.)—Description and travel. 4. Hartford (Conn.)—Pictorial works. I. Shepard, William, 1954– II. Title.
F104.H3C67 2003
974.6'3—dc22

                    2003024014

Printed in the United States of America by Walsworth Publishing Company

Table of
Contents

Acknowledgments

I am obliged to many people who have given me encouragement, suggestions, and information for this project.

This book would not be possible without the talents of photographer William Shepard. His constant patience and professionalism have brought wondrous results. This is his book as much as mine.

I would also like to thank the many historians and librarians who helped me with my extensive research from the Noah Webster House Museum, the Connecticut Historical Society, the Connecticut State Library, and the Hartford Public Library.

I especially would like to thank Wilson Faude, Jack Hale, Robert Prill, and Donna Fuss for their interviews. Special thanks also to Nancy Thody and Diana Lyn Cote for their many suggestions for the book.

This book would not be possible without the love and support of my husband, David Cornelio.

I dedicate this book to my uncle, Charles Meli.

Introduction

Elizabeth Park is a magical place. It must be. I have never seen two words create such a twinkle in people's eyes and an immediate unsolicited account of a fond bygone memory. "I loved watching the goldfish in the pond." "I used to ice-skate there as a child." "I was married in Elizabeth Park." "My family always picnicked in the park." "I rode my bike there every day." I also have fond memories of Elizabeth Park. My uncle, Charles Meli, was past park superintendent of Hartford. We enjoyed many family gatherings at the park.

How shocked I was to learn that no book about Elizabeth Park had ever been written! I became determined to see it done in time for the Rose Garden Centennial.

Researching Elizabeth Park's rich history was an adventure. I never thought an innocent little park could create such controversy over the years! Elizabeth Park's biggest troubles surround the fact that the park straddles two municipalities. The mystery is how

Elizabeth Park became divided between Hartford and West Hartford. Some local historians blame the water company for changing the town line during the border disputes of the 1870s. The new border divided the Pond Estate between the two municipalities. When Charles Pond chose the City of Hartford to inherit his estate for a park that resided mostly in another town, it created the unique situation that remains today.

Mother Nature also had her share of controversy! Bill Shepard had many photography challenges. Knowing he had to shoot all the pictures during the previous year, 2003 had the worst weather, even by New England standards. First, we had the harshest winter in years. Winter came early and roses did not have time to reach full dormancy. Massive winterkill resulted. A good portion of a spring meeting of the Connecticut Rose Society was devoted to the testimonials of seasoned rosarians concerning their losses. Many rose plants had to be replaced at Elizabeth Park that spring. Then came the constant chilling rains that did not let up until the end of June. Elizabeth Park relies heavily on volunteers to weed their rose beds. It rained virtually every weekend for three months, delaying work. When the sun finally burst through, we found many rose beds with weeds as high as the roses! This was a huge challenge for Bill and his camera. But, despite all the horrible weather, many of the

roses dried out beautifully and were picture perfect. The annuals and perennials also "rose" to the challenge and produced spectacular displays.

My goal in writing this book is to create a keepsake for the visitor. The book will be a current reminder of a recent visit to Elizabeth Park as well as a travel into its past. Although the Rose Garden is primarily featured, the other botanical aspects of Elizabeth Park are given much deserved attention. Most importantly, the book demonstrates a vibrant place created for all people to enjoy. Parks are essential to cities. Hopefully, this book will create a renewed appreciation of parks and the desire to advocate for these special places.

The Park and
Its Mission
1

Elizabeth Park is considered the "garden park" of the Hartford Parks system. Although most of the Hartford parks developed in the nineteenth century were previous estates, Charles M. Pond's estate had the largest varieties of plants and flowers. Theodore Wirth, first park superintendent, took advantage of the existing flora when designing Elizabeth Park. Flowers and shrubs were arranged in highly ornamental displays similar to a botanic garden. John Charles Olmsted, representing the Olmsted firm that designed the grounds, described their vision as a "gentleman's suburban residence playground."[1]

Elizabeth Park featured formal carpet bedding that changed each year, a Sunken Garden with turfed steps, a Perennial Garden, a Rock Garden, a Fernery, and the famous Rose Garden. Currently, Elizabeth Park also

has an Herb Garden, Heritage Rose Garden, and the Dahlia Garden. The Sunken Garden and Fernery are lost to history, but the other gardens remain to give Elizabeth Park its continuing status as Hartford's "gem."

Today, Elizabeth Park still provides pleasure to garden enthusiasts. Rose Weekend in June attracts large crowds. However, people also come to Elizabeth Park for its recreational

Opposite Page: 'Pink Peace' hybrid tea rose

Below: A volunteer weeder spruces up a rose bed.

9

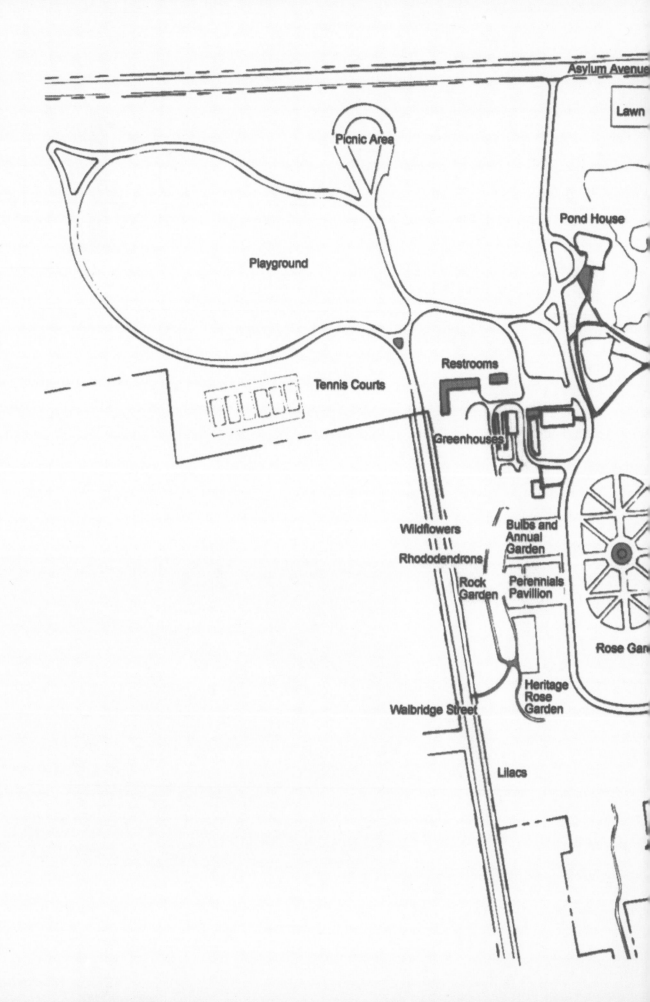

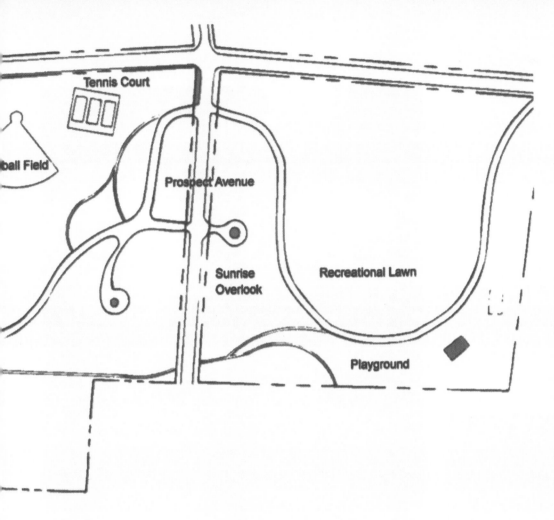

Map of
Elizabeth Park

Right: Elizabeth Park entrance

Below: Greenhouse plants ready for transplanting

and leisure activities. Bicyclists, dog walkers, sunbathers, sports players, and picnickers can be seen any day of the week.

Elizabeth Park is under the care of the Hartford Parks Department with help from a volunteer community organization known as the Friends of Elizabeth Park. They work very closely together to care for the park. The City of Hartford maintains Elizabeth Park, employing the staff gardeners. The Friends of Elizabeth Park's main mission is to raise funds to renovate and improve the gardens and buildings, purchase plants and supplies, and increase the awareness and enjoyment of Elizabeth Park. They sponsor a series of tours and educational workshops that are free and open to the public. The Friends of Elizabeth Park also help support the city's work with volunteers. These volunteers can be seen weeding their assigned flowerbeds throughout the park. Since Elizabeth Park is a regional attraction, the combination of efforts from these municipal and community groups has been especially beneficial to the park.

Robert Prill, gardening foreman, carefully oversees Elizabeth Park.

THE EARLY YEARS

Elizabeth Park was born from the American Park Movement of the mid-nineteenth century. Parks designed during the American Park Movement had a much different purpose from the creation of the typical New England Town Commons that were used as grazing and work areas for residents. It was a direct response to the negative influences of the Industrial Revolution. Many people viewed urbanization and industrialization as a change for the worse for American life. Factory work separated individuals from country settings and created a blighted landscape in the cities. Transcendentalist reformers pushed for the creation of open, natural settings that offered relief to families. Landscapers of the American Park Movement chose the pastoral landscape as the best compromise of achieving wilderness inside a city. Varieties of trees, large reflecting ponds, and wide walkways created an idealized agrarian setting. Buildings were few and airy in design, often without walls. Sculpture was also restricted to disassociate the movement from European aristocratic formal gardens. These parks were meant to provide a democratic setting where all classes of society could interact.[1]

Opposite Page: Clematis

Below: The Elizabeth Park Rose Garden was created as a respite for city residents.
(Connecticut Historical Society)

Elizabeth Aldrich Pond, for whom Elizabeth Park is named
(CONNECTICUT HISTORICAL SOCIETY)

Frederick Law Olmsted, a pioneer of the movement, was born in Hartford, Connecticut in 1822. Bushnell Park, created in 1853 in Hartford, reflected Olmsted's philosophies. Bushnell Park replaced a filthy, smelly, congested slum area that was often regarded as a "hell on earth."[2] The significant improvement to the city that Bushnell Park provided led the way to the creation of more parks in Hartford.

The Reverend Francis Goodwin, an enthusiast of the American Park Movement, is regarded as the Father of Hartford Parks. He was a prominent Hartford clergyman and a cousin of J. P. Morgan.[3] Goodwin was instrumental in convincing wealthy Hartford citizens to will their estates to create a Hartford park system. His philanthropic successes, coupled with Olmsted's design philosophies, influenced the creation of a "Rain of Parks": the largest acquisition of land for a park system in the history of Hartford. Between August 30, 1894 and November 14, 1895, five major parks were bequeathed or purchased to add nearly twelve hundred acres of parkland to the City of Hartford. These parks included Elizabeth Park, Colt Park, Pope Park, Keney Park, and Riverside Park.

Elizabeth Park was the first park to be bequeathed during the Rain of Parks period. The Reverend Francis Goodwin's first philanthropic success was the gift of the Charles M. Pond Estate to the City of Hartford in 1894. Pond's stunning generosity prompted other wealthy Hartford citizens to bequeath their lands to form the Rain of Parks.[4]

Charles M. Pond was a flamboyant character of the Gilded Age. He was born in New York City on February 5, 1837 into a wealthy family. He studied business at Trinity College in Hartford from 1854 to 1858 but never achieved his degree. He left to join the family business of the Hartford and New Haven Railroad where he became treasurer. Then, in

1868, he entered the banking industry when he founded the Hartford Trust Company and became its first president. Pond also served in the Connecticut legislature and became state treasurer in 1870.

Charles M. Pond purchased the Prospect Hill Farm in 1847 from his father, Charles F. Pond. It was a ninety-six-acre parcel of land that began at present-day Prospect Avenue and continued westward. Here is where Charles Pond and his wife Elizabeth Aldrich Pond set up residence for the rest of their lives. Pond was a sharp businessman, but he enjoyed high living at the Prospect Hill estate. He built a twenty-room, three-story mansion with Corinthian columns and wide porches. Many of the rooms had carved marble fireplaces. Pond loved horses and indulged in one of the most popular pastimes of the wealthy at that time: horse trotting races. He was famous for breeding many purebred trotters that he raced

Charles M. Pond, benefactor of Elizabeth Park
(Connecticut State Library)

on the estate. One horse, called Clingstone, was a sensation known as the "trotting demon."[5] Pond was also fond of guns. It is said that he summoned his laborers to the evening meal by firing a shotgun from his rear veranda.

Pond had originally planned to leave his estate for the care of inebriates, but the Reverend Francis Goodwin convinced him to bequeath it to Hartford for its park system. He left the entire Prospect Hill estate to Hartford and $160,000 for additional land purchase and maintenance. He requested that the park be named after his wife Elizabeth.[6]

Pond died on August 30, 1894, from complications of spinal meningitis, at his Prospect Hill estate. His obituary hailed Pond as a talented and successful business leader and politician. It described how he died with his sister lovingly by his side. The Reverend Francis Goodwin presided over the funeral, and Pond was buried in the family vault at Spring Grove Cemetery.[7]

The original residence of Charles and Elizabeth Pond was demolished in 1956.
(CONNECTICUT HISTORICAL SOCIETY)

It was a harmonious family picture until Pond's siblings learned about the contents of his will. Charles M. Pond had no children, and his brother, Anson Pond, especially expected to inherit his estate. Anson Pond immediately contested the will and enlisted the support of his sister, Clara Pond Porter. The Pond siblings began a smear campaign to discredit their brother's actions. The litigation created a sensation. Suddenly, this well-respected businessman and politician was depicted by his siblings as an alcoholic and morphine addict and not of sound mind when he wrote his will. The members of the Court of Common Council, especially two youthful members, Isidore Wise and Thomas W. Gunshanan, valiantly fought to retain its bequest.[8]

The trial appeared in the *Hartford Courant* almost like the script of a play with each part recorded word for word. Witnesses described Pond's constant drunken state. Others described Pond's addiction to morphine, a drug that he allegedly shared with his dog Trumps; the dog, it was said, would come to Pond regularly for his morphine dose. And, there was the extensive testimony about his indulgence in spiritualism.

18

Witnesses described Pond's activities with mediums and the Ouija board.[9] In contrast, Anson was a relatively successful playwright. His most famous play, *Her Atonement*, was about the Grand Army of the Republic. During the trial deliberations, members of the GAR came to Hartford in huge numbers to demonstrate support for Anson Pond.[10]

Judge Eggleston represented the Pond siblings, while Judge Thayer presided over the trial. On March 15, 1896, the jury decided that Pond's last will was invalid, giving the estate to the Pond siblings. The jury felt the will had not been properly executed and Pond was influenced by outsiders due to an unsound mind. But Judge Thayer considered the verdict "absurd" and accused the jury of being influenced by outsiders and showing bias.[11] Two weeks later, after going over the extensive testimony, Judge Thayer set the verdict aside. He argued that the jury verdict was decided against the evidence. And rather than have the family appeal to a higher court, it was determined that a new trial would take place as if the original trial had never happened.[12] Finally, in 1897, a compromise was made between the family and the City of Hartford. Hartford retained the estate but accepted a smaller monetary amount, $105,000, for its upkeep.[13]

Theodore Wirth was hired as superintendent of Elizabeth Park in 1896. He was a Swiss landscape architect who had worked with Frederick Law Olmsted, creator of Central Park in New York City. Charles M. Pond was a lover of trees and flowers and had many unique species on his estate. It was this special interest that set Elizabeth Park apart from the other Hartford parks in the design phase. Rather than create a pastoral park in the manner of other parks designed during the American Park Movement, it was decided to create a garden park for the enjoyment of the masses. Elizabeth Park can now claim the oldest municipal rose garden in the United States due to this unique design decision. Thereafter, Wirth became a strong supporter of

Theodore Wirth was Elizabeth Park's first park superintendent. He began design of the grounds and gardens in 1897.

George A. Parker succeeded Wirth as park superintendent. He was responsible for adding recreational areas to Elizabeth Park.
(Connecticut State Library)

park designs that supported playgrounds and recreational areas for families.[14]

Unfortunately, Wirth's tenure as Hartford superintendent of Elizabeth Park was short-lived. In 1906, he accepted a similar position in Minneapolis, Minnesota where his best work was accomplished. So outstanding was his design of the Minneapolis Park System that planners flocked to the city from all over the country to view his work. Elizabeth Park was fortunate to have as its founding landscaper a man of such innovation and talent.

Mr. George A. Parker, originally superintendent of Keney Park, became superintendent of all Hartford parks, including Elizabeth Park, in 1906. The New England Park Association was conceived in March 1898 by Parker and took a leadership role in park management. And, it was during Parker's tenure as park superintendent that he radically altered his philosophies of park management. American Park Movement designs reflected natural, country settings. A border of shrubs and trees was planted at the edges of parks to hide streets and lights. The idea was to give visitors the illusion that they weren't even in a city. Unfortunately, certain city residents misused these public places. Vagrants and drunks began frequenting the parks at night. Many couples used the parks for their sexual escapades. Vandalism was rampant. Park superintendents had to rethink park management to counter these negative activities. Parker had surrounding shrubs uprooted and lighting installed in all the Hartford parks. He also decided that citizens needed constructive activities while visiting parks. Thus began the concept of providing recreational activities within parks. Ball fields, playgrounds, and picnic areas were created.[15]

Parker did compromise in the design of Elizabeth Park by segregating recreational areas from the formal gardens. Playing fields and picnic areas were situated near streets and away from the garden so that the activities of one would not conflict with the other. Parker also established Elizabeth Park as the first test garden for the American Rose Society in 1912, setting it apart from other strictly recreational parks.

George H. Hollister followed as Hartford's superintendent of parks in 1926. He had the longest tenure of all the park superintendents of Hartford. He stepped down at the age of seventy-two, due to Hartford's mandatory retirement age of seventy and the refusal of the City Council to grant him another one-year extension of employment. Still, he continued as a consultant for many years after.[16] Mr. Hollister was born in Medina, Ohio in 1882 and graduated from Connecticut Agricultural College in 1902 with an AB in agriculture. In 1909, he joined the local park system as a forester in Keney Park. He was promoted to assistant

The rose arches of Elizabeth Park in this vintage picture are the same roses that are growing today, a century later.
(Connecticut Historical Society)

21

Looking west from Elizabeth Park, the suburban streets of West Hartford did not exist in 1900. Stately homes sprung up after the development of the park.
(Connecticut Historical Society)

superintendent of Hartford parks in 1921 and superintendent in 1926. He was former president of American Institute of Park Executives and helped reactivate the New England Park Association in 1916. Hollister was made an honorary life member of the New England Park Association in 1951. He was also a University of Connecticut trustee from 1927–1943 and had a dormitory named after him. Mr. Hollister coined the term "Rain of Parks" in a paper he published about the history of the Hartford Parks system.[17]

Hollister's most significant decision was his recommendation in 1952 to demolish the old Pond Estate House. Pond had built the house in 1846 when he acquired the estate from his father. When the park first opened, many visitors rested on the verandas and in the first-floor parlor. The second floor was used as the park superintendent's office, and the first floor was used for meetings. Unfortunately, no major work had been done to the house since the city had taken over the estate as a park. The deteriorating condition of the house made it less and less attractive to groups for meetings and functions. The original furniture had not been saved and was long gone. The floors sagged, and patrons complained of a constant musty smell. Hollister felt that the cost of operation was making it more of a liability than a benefit to the public.[18]

After an analysis in May 1952 by the City Council, it was determined that it would cost $16,814 to restore the first floor only and make it structurally sound. Hollister was pressing for a new Pond House structure to be built near the pond.[19] A battle began with the objection of the Hartford Elderlies Association, a group of senior citizen park advocates formed by George A. Parker. They stormed a City Council meeting and made a convincing argument for saving the Pond Estate House.[20] The council voted to look further into the matter. In July 1953, the City Council voted to repair the Pond Estate House beginning in November 1953 and finishing by April 1954. City Manager Carlton Sharpe appropriated money in the next year's budget for repairs that were now estimated at $18,000.[21] The repairs never began. Despite a nationwide economic boom in

The sheepfold was converted to a skate house by 1910 when it was no longer considered practical to keep sheep for the lawns.
(CONNECTICUT STATE LIBRARY)

23

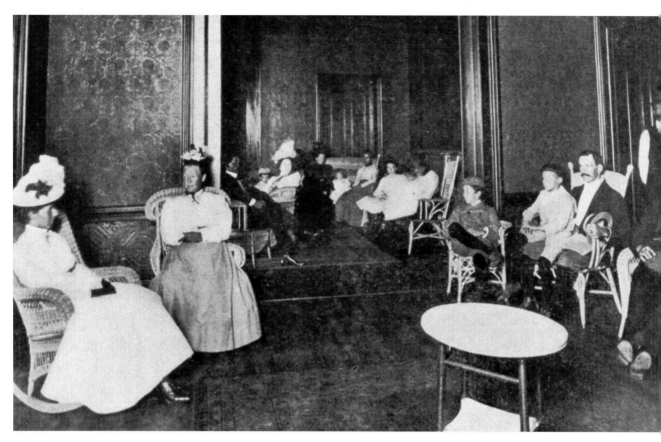

Early visitors rest on the veranda of the Pond Estate House.
(CONNECTICUT STATE LIBRARY)

the 1950s, Hartford was experiencing budget deficits. Hollister successfully delayed the project until his retirement in 1954.

THE MIDDLE YEARS

In 1954, Everett A. Piester succeeded George Hollister as park superintendent. He had begun working for the Hartford Parks Department in 1927, almost as long as Hollister himself. He received his BA in landscaping from Cornell University and an MA in landscape design from the University of Michigan. Piester was one of the most active and intellectual park superintendents of his time. He was a member of the American Institute of Park Executives and the Royal Horticultural Society, among many other park and forestry associations. A past secretary of the American Association of Botanic Gardens and former president of the Midwest Society of Landscape Architects, he also was a certified rosarian and official rose test judge. Piester also found time to be a regular contributor to the *New York Times* gardening column.[22]

Having worked so long with Hollister, Piester also believed that the Pond Estate House should be demolished. He took up Hollister's cause to build a new Pond House. Piester argued that the house used forty-five tons of coal a year for heating and was used mainly by fifteen Elderlies for their five meetings per year.[23] After much delay, the Elderlies lost their fight. The City Council voted to raze the Pond Estate House and appropriated $100,000 to build a new skate house and concession stand. The house was demolished in July 1956. Ironically, the decision to scrap a historically significant building came back to haunt the City Council.

In 1958, work was serenely being done on the new Pond House. Hartford had secured bonds to cover the $100,000 expense of the building and it was almost complete. City Manager Carlton Sharpe was overseeing the project when Mayor James Kinsella suddenly accused him of authorizing an expenditure for an architect, two years earlier, without the approval of the City Council. The amount in dispute was a mere five percent of the total cost but Kinsella used it as an affront to the city's charter. Again, Elizabeth Park was the center of a major city dispute.[24]

A school in Hartford holds its annual Field Day in Elizabeth Park.
(CONNECTICUT STATE LIBRARY)

The City Charter Committee accused Kinsella of discrediting Sharpe in an attempt to change the manager form of government.[25] Many citizens saw the real issue as the control of city funds, and the investigation tore Hartford into two camps. Kinsella's supporters felt the City Charter was threatened. Sharpe's supporters felt the issue was insignificant and did not justify such a huge protest. Despite the small expenditure, Kinsella filed official charges against Sharpe and called a special session of the

City Council.[26] During proceedings, Sharpe defended his actions by stating that the architect fee in question was for consulting work and was approved by the Finance Department and city auditor.[27] Sharpe's lawyer stated that the City Charter was vague about funding for consultants.[28] A public hearing in December 1958 attracted hundreds of people. Sharpe conceded that he may have erred in judgment concerning the expenditure, but he assured the City Council that the work was exemplary and a credit to the Pond House project. Sharpe also stated that he never received any written opinion by the city lawyer that he could not hire a consultant.[29]

An editorial by the *Hartford Courant* in 1959 summed up the investigation as too trivial to create such division in the city government. It was more a trial for the validity of the position of city manager. Ironically, the mayor was also accused of not following the charter, which he so stringently defended, in the process of dismissing a city employee.[30] In the end, the City Council voted to censure City Manager Sharpe for violating the City Charter. Some City Council members objected to the severity of the resolution, citing that Sharpe had no evil intent in his actions and there was no personal gain. The resolution was negatively viewed by the public. At the January 1959 censoring meeting, Kinsella defended his actions as "upholding the law of the charter" and added that "the violent, venomous, and often obscene telephone calls to his home have not been pleasant."[31]

Mr. Everett J. Pyle briefly succeeded Mr. Piester as park super-intendent in 1961. He graduated with a BA from the University of Massachusetts in landscape architecture. Pyle began with the Hartford Parks Department in 1936. He was well known as a turf specialist and oversaw the golf course at Goodwin Park. He was not a rosarian, however, and did not give any special attention to Elizabeth Park. He left the position of park superintendent in 1964 to become director of Parks and Recreation.[32]

Mr. Victor J. Jarm succeeded Mr. Pyle as park superintendent in 1964. He began with the Hartford Parks Department in 1950. Mr. Jarm's specialty was forestry and he was the city forester for many years. Mr. Jarm was the first park superintendent to recognize the decline in park attendance. He attributed this phenomenon to the advent of television. In older days, people would venture from their homes for entertainment rather than be entertained at home. Jarm created programs to encourage more citizens back into the parks. His goal was to create "peaceful park activities by working closely with neighborhood groups." He advocated park concerts, picnic activities, and playing fields. Mr. Jarm succeeded Mr. Pyle as director of Parks and Recreation in 1969.[33]

Charles Meli was the first park superintendent to truly devote his entire life and career to Elizabeth Park. Born and raised in Hartford, he began as a common laborer in 1937 after he graduated from high school. He worked as a gardener exclusively in Elizabeth Park until 1946. His career was interrupted by World War II when he joined the Army and fought in the Pacific. He was promoted to sergeant and decorated for valor. He took advantage of the GI Bill to pursue a career in horticulture and graduated from the University of Connecticut in 1950 with a BA in landscape design. Meli's background was different from his predecessors, but through devotion and hard work, he gained the respect of park administrators and eventually found himself at the top.

Charles Meli began his commitment to Elizabeth Park by becoming certified as a rose test judge. He was forever after called Mr. Rose by city employees. In 1957 he became the city's landscape architect. From 1958 to 1961, he studied architectural design at the University of Hartford. Then he became city forester in 1964. During this time, he remained the city's rosarian and oversaw the rose test program at

Tom Queeno, gardener foreman of Elizabeth Park, waters plants in the greenhouse for the annual Spring Flower Show in 1974.
(Hartford Public Library)

27

Queen candidates for the Greater Hartford Queen of Roses in 1973. Front to back: Anita Davis, Nancy Bossler, Linda Pearle, Frances Monahan, Stella Laskowski, Patrice Murphy, and Robon Benard.
(HARTFORD PUBLIC LIBRARY)

Elizabeth Park. In 1969, he was promoted to the position of park superintendent.[34]

Meli began promoting programs at Elizabeth Park right away. He created the first Nine Days of Roses Festival in 1969 to promote family participation at Elizabeth Park. It would culminate with a Rose Queen pageant. The spring and fall flower shows, a park tradition, were at the height of their popularity and drew huge crowds. But Meli also oversaw Elizabeth Park in the worst of times.

It is not a unique situation for a park to straddle two municipalities, but the Yankee aversion to regionalism has created unnecessary problems for Elizabeth Park. It is still a mystery how Elizabeth Park came to be under two juridictions. West Hartford was incorporated in 1854, after the purchase of the Pond Estate. Why the lines would be drawn to divide someone's estate is unknown.

Again, financial problems and budget cuts stressed the workforce maintaining Hartford's parks. In 1975, Hartford officials declared that the rose gardens would be closed and plowed under if they did not receive financial help from the suburbs. The City Council asked West Hartford to help by providing ten percent of the total cost to maintain Elizabeth Park: $30,000. However, no help came from West Hartford or any other suburb.[35]

In late 1975, the City Council began a controversial program to charge an admission fee to the Rose Gardens. Recognizing that most visitors were from the suburbs, the City Council decided to charge one dollar to any adult nonresident and twenty-five cents to children of nonresidents. Jarm estimated revenue from the admission fee to be about $57,000 based on past park attendance figures.[36] The plan was implemented in 1976. Residents had to register with the Hartford Parks Department and cards were issued. The Rose Gardens were roped off and a booth with a ticket seller was installed. It was a disastrous plan. Visitors to the Rose Gardens dropped off from an average of 100,000 people to 3,000. Bus tours dropped from approximately forty to exactly three. The city lost $248 after paying its ticket sellers. Visitors paying the fee displayed a "negative and sometimes belligerent attitude." Noticeably, usage of other facilities at the park did not decline. The fee was suspended in the fall of 1976.[37]

Other ideas were brought to the City Council to support the Rose Garden. The city manager recommended that each town in the capital region sponsor a section of the Rose Garden for $100 to $500 per year. Each section would bear the name of the sponsor who could then hold special events in the Rose Garden. But still, there was no response from the suburbs.[38]

Hartford residents register at the park for free access to the rose gardens. The plan to charge nonresidents to view the rose gardens to raise money was a complete failure.
(HARTFORD PUBLIC LIBRARY)

29

Neighborhood children raise money to save the rose garden in 1976.
(Hartford Public Library)

In 1977, the City Council again proposed closing the Rose Garden. City Councilor Nicholas R. Carbone led the initiative stating, "If we can't get regional support, we should contemplate closing the garden."[39] West Hartford became alarmed at the seriousness of the Hartford proposal and suddenly pledged $1,500 for Elizabeth Park. Talks began between Hartford and West Hartford to create a "workable division of labor and expenses." The West Hartford town manager recognized the interest of West Hartford citizens in the park since much of it resides in their town. By the spring of 1978, talks between the two municipalities had produced nothing.[40] Former West Hartford Mayor Ellsworth S. Grant tried to entice West Hartford to pledge $10,000 to the park by promising to match the gift from a private source.[41] Despite favorable responses from West Hartford residents, Mayor Anne P. Streeter warned that the West Hartford charter did not allow any gifts larger than $500 to anybody without West Hartford representation.[42] Hartford responded by drafting a proposal for a six-member committee with three representatives from each municipality to oversee Elizabeth Park.[43] The response from the West Hartford government was tepid.

Realizing West Hartford was not going to help save Elizabeth Park with financial support, Hartford tried another tactic. They applied for a federal grant of $1.5 million for capital improvements to Elizabeth Park.[44] Because Elizabeth Park has the unfortunate circumstance of straddling two municipalities, a joint committee was required to be eligible for the grant.[45] By the winter of 1978, West Hartford finally endorsed a plan for a joint committee. But, after all that effort, the grant was rejected by the Department of the Interior.[46]

THE LATER YEARS

The City of Hartford also cut expenses by dismantling the Parks Department. Purely maintenance activities, such as the work of the gardeners, were placed under the Public Works Department. Recreational activities were placed under the Department of Human Services. This greatly diminished the stature of the position of park superintendent and lowered the priority of parks by the city. Charles Meli retired in 1983 as the last park superintendent under the old system.

In typical American fashion, when government becomes gridlocked on an issue, private citizens take action. In 1977, the Friends of Elizabeth Park was formed. Ironically, most of its initial members were from West Hartford. By 1978, the group had collected more than ten thousand dollars in donations, including over two hundred rose plants from Jackson & Perkins. They pledged one thousand new rose plants for fifty rose beds.[47] Later, Friends of Elizabeth Park got a huge boost when they received a one million dollar endowment that became known as the Ethel F. Donaghue Trust. This enabled the group to direct their efforts to the

Mrs. Richard Stula purchases roses from Mr. Kevin Porter at the Gift Shop in Rockville, Connecticut to support the Hartford Times *drive to benefit Elizabeth Park's Rose Garden in 1975.*
(HARTFORD PUBLIC LIBRARY)

other gardens in Elizabeth Park, including the restoration of the Perennial and Rock Gardens. Charles Meli and Victor J. Jarm were founding members of the Friends of Elizabeth Park and worked closely with the group to guide various projects. The efforts of the Friends of Elizabeth Park were rewarded when, on March 10, 1983, Elizabeth Park became enrolled on the National Register of Historic Places.[48] Another highlight in Elizabeth Park's history was its designation by the All-American Rose Selections as the Most Outstanding Rose Garden of 1990.

As the millennium approached, a new controversy enveloped Elizabeth Park. The problem of the park straddling two municipalities came to a head. The park is considered part of the Hartford Parks system, and Hartford maintains the park with tax revenue from its citizens. West Hartford retains zoning control of the areas of Elizabeth Park within its town limits but its citizens don't contribute any money for the park's upkeep. Pulitzer Prize-winning writer Virginia Groark summarized the situation best in a *Hartford Courant* article on November 18, 2001.[49]

The controversy surrounds the operation of a restaurant in the Pond House at Elizabeth Park. Again, the City of Hartford had allowed a structure in Elizabeth Park to deteriorate badly. And again, the city struggled to find funds for its repair. In a similar situation to the Pond Estate House, the deteriorated condition of the building discouraged groups from using it for functions. So, the City of Hartford came up with an idea: allow the Friends of Elizabeth Park to manage the Pond House. If they could find a high-quality restaurant to rent space in the Pond House, they could keep eighty percent of the net income from rent and banquet proceeds to continue their efforts at improving and maintaining Elizabeth Park. Finally, Elizabeth Park would have a way to generate income for itself and the days of fiscal crisis could end.

The Pond House space was renovated in 1996 with the help of private, Hartford, and state money. The permit to renovate the Pond House was approved by the West Hartford Town Planning and Zoning Commission. The restaurant opened in May 1999. Many citizens were delighted with the new restaurant, but others felt it was too upscale and expensive for the average park visitor. When the restaurant applied for a liquor permit, neighbors began to object.[50]

The raucous town meetings divided the two municipalities and the citizens of West Hartford themselves. An agreement between the two jurisdictions on permissable activities

was enacted in 2001. It was not to the satisfaction of eleven neighbors. On August 19, 2002, Superior Court Judge Robert Beach granted intervenor status to eleven West Hartford neighbors who had brought a suit arguing against the Pond House activities.[51] The decision severely limits the park's ability to raise money for its upkeep.

John Kehoe became park superintendent in 2003 and has many challenges ahead. The Pond House dispute is still pending. Perhaps Elizabeth Park will always be at the center of controversy. It is a municipal park, but it attracts visitors from far outside Hartford's borders. Restricting the park's ability to raise money for itself will assuredly contribute to the demise of the park's treasured gardens. Entrance fees have not worked in the past, but other enterprises should be considered. Most state and national parks generate income through commercial activities such as group tours, gift shops and food concessions. Upgrading Elizabeth Park's status as a regional park could ensure its survival.

Left: The Honorable Eddie A. Perez, mayor of Hartford. The City of Hartford owns and maintains Elizabeth Park.

Above: The Honorable Jonathan Harris, mayor of West Hartford. Elizabeth Park resides mostly in West Hartford.

Elizabeth Park
Rose Garden
3

The Rose Garden at Elizabeth Park is the indisputable main attraction of the park. Thousands of visitors flock to the park every June to view the spectacular display. Elizabeth Park includes the oldest and third largest public rose garden in the United States. It now contains fifteen thousand roses of eight hundred different varieties. The present site used to be the racetrack for Charles Pond's thoroughbred trotters. But I think everyone will agree that a rose garden is an excellent alternative for the site!

Rose bed selections are determined by the head rosarian of Elizabeth Park. Those varieties that don't survive New England weather are replaced with other roses. Some rose beds are planted with varieties requested by the donors of particular beds. Also, a certain number of rose beds are planted with AARS winners to demonstrate new varieties to the viewing public before the roses become available for sale the following year.

Theodore Wirth began by planning and planting a one and a half acre Rose Garden in 1896. It contained one thousand rose plants of one hundred different varieties. It was moved

*Opposite Page: 'Love',
a grandiflora rose*

*Below: 'Baronne Prevost', a hybrid
perpetual rose*

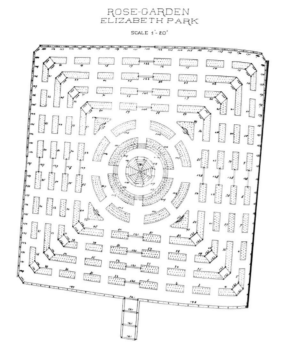

ROSE-GARDEN
ELIZABETH PARK
SCALE 1'-20'

and expanded to two and a half acres in 1904. He wanted a new area with better drainage and better access to the park's drives. This included an elevated rustic summer house that provided views of the entire Rose Garden from all directions. The new arrangements of rose beds and walkways accommodated larger crowds, which could then distribute themselves evenly in all directions. A system of water pipes was arranged to reach every part of the Rose Garden. One hundred thirty-two beds of roses were planted with one rose variety featured en masse in each individual rose bed. The majority of the roses were hybrid perpetuals, and those that remain have not been moved since they were first planted in 1903.[1]

Wirth created a Rose Garden with a decidedly Continental feel. The development and maintenance of a rose garden using public funds was a mid-

Above: Theodore Wirth's original plan for the rose garden in the 1904 Annual Park Report

Right: An aerial view of the rose garden with the first rose test garden to the left. A second semi-circular section was added in 1936 to round out the appearance of the rose garden.
(CONNECTICUT HISTORICAL SOCIETY)

nineteenth-century European idea. The multi-variety rose garden was the inspiration of Empress Josephine of France. She had two hundred fifty rose varieties in her garden in 1799, including varieties from Japan and China. French soldiers returned from war campaigns with rose specimens for the empress. The Elizabeth Park Rose Garden with its arched pathways was created before the famous 1912 Roseraie in the Parc de Bagatelle in Paris, France. The garden, with its eight arched pathways emanating from the center like the spokes of a wheel, resembles the botanical garden in Padua, Italy created in 1545.[2]

Wirth's original design for the rose arches remains today. All the walks are arched over by seventy-eight single wood or iron arches. One variety of rose is used in each walkway to create a unified look. 'Red Crimson Rambler' and 'Excelsa' roses are used for the crosswalks, while white and pink 'Dorothy Perkins' roses are used for the diagonal walks. All the roses growing on the arches are original plantings from a century ago! The

Eight rows of rose arches emanate from the center rustic summer house like the spokes of a wheel.

The elevated rustic summer house at the center of the rose garden provides views in every direction.

walks intersect at a rustic summer house built on a circular platform to enhance views of the entire Rose Garden. Although there are larger municipal rose gardens in the United States, few possess such an exceptional design.[3]

It was during George Parker's administration that Elizabeth Park first became a test garden for the American Rose Society in 1912. It became the first official rose test garden in the United States. A one-half-acre semicircular area was added to the south side of the Rose Garden for this purpose. It contained approximately 3,100 roses of the new hybrid tea varieties so well suited to the New England climate.

In 1936, at the request of the American Rose Society, another semicircular test garden area was added to the Rose Garden to round out its appearance. This addition brought the number of rose plants to its present-day number of fifteen thousand plants with eight hundred varieties. It was planted in preparation for the American Rose Society's

Miniature rose 'Lemon Drop'

annual convention to be held in Hartford in 1937. Theodore Wirth was honored at this convention with the society's Gold Medal of Honor for his work as the Father of the American Rose Garden.

The preparations for the convention were almost a disaster by a new threat never before encountered in Connecticut rose gardens: the Japanese beetle. Introduced into the United States from Asia on nursery plants around 1916, the beetle first made its appearance in Connecticut around 1930. The Japanese beetles were not a serious threat until 1936. Panicked city leaders watched as the ravenous insects destroyed most of the trees of Riverside Park and began on the gardens of Elizabeth Park. Their hard shells seemed impervious to foliar sprays.[4] Finally, a plan to soak the ground with thirty tons of lead arsenate to kill the grubs was enacted. $10,000 was appropriated from the Common Council. The spray was applied by WPA labor as well as park staff over several weeks. The arsenic compound was pumped through power sprays and washed down with water to kill the larvae while still in the ground.[5] The park plants, especially the roses, were saved, and the convention took place the following summer with much success.

'Orange Dream' is a hybrid tea rose.

Originally, all the rose varieties were hybrid perpetuals. Many of these centennial survivors are not available anywhere else in the United States. Over the years, the rose beds have been replanted with many of the newer varieties: hybrid teas, grandifloras, floribundas, and miniatures. The Rose Garden received a substantial renovation in the 1980s from the Friends of Elizabeth Park. This community organization was created in 1977 when the Rose Garden was

Above: 'Knockout' is a new shrub rose variety that is highly disease resistant.

Right: 'Blueberry Hill', a floribunda rose, is named for its unusual color.

threatened with extinction because adequate funds could not be raised for its upkeep. The Friends of Elizabeth Park, however, managed to raise enough funds and secure an endowment to preserve the roses and all the gardens of Elizabeth Park.

Today, the Rose Garden is in its best condition in a half-century. It continues to attract large crowds of visitors, wedding participants, photographers and painters.

HERITAGE ROSE GARDEN

Elizabeth Park also has a smaller rose garden of exclusively old garden varieties. This garden was created in 1912. It is best viewed in early June, since most of the roses only bloom once per season. The visitor will see the centifolia, alba, gallica, and damask varieties that are rarely grown elsewhere. One rose, *Rosa sericea pterancantha*, is as old as the dinosaurs. It can be easily recognized by the huge razor-sharp thorns that line its canes from top to bottom.

Above: 'Sheila's Perfume', a hybrid tea rose, is highly fragrant.

Left: 'Scentimental', a hybrid tea rose, is known for its candy-striped appearance.

41

HISTORY OF THE ROSE

Roses have been part of human culture since the beginning of mankind. Fossil remains of roses have been discovered that are thirty-five million years old. The Greek poet Sappho called the rose the "Queen of Flowers" 2,500 years ago when the only roses were the simple wild roses. Roses are also mentioned in Homer's *Iliad* and *Odyssey* and the historian Herodotus mentions King Midas's rose garden in *Phrygia*. Thousands of miles to the east, Confucius wrote about the extensive rose plantings in the Peking Imperial Gardens. Asian coins printed four thousand years ago bear rose motifs. Rose decorations have been found in Assyrian and Babylonian ruins, Cretan frescos, and Egyptian mummy crypts. Renaissance Flemish and Dutch still-life paintings often depict portraits of roses.

Above: 'The McCartney Rose', a hybrid tea rose, is named for singer-songwriter Paul McCartney who commissioned its creation.

Right: Miniature rose 'Magic Carousel' is especially dramatic in a group.

*The rose arches
in full bloom*

At the height of the Roman Empire, the rose was prevalent in family gardens. The flowers were used in weddings and funerals and at parties as well as festival days. Wealthy Romans bathed in rose water, wore rose garlands, ate foods with rose petals and drank rose wine. Medicines were used from rose petals, hips, and seeds. Even today, rose hips are considered a good source of vitamin C. A huge rose industry developed in Egypt, a one-time colony of Rome, where the winters were mild.

A pink alba rose

As the ancient Roman Empire collapsed, the newly converted Roman Christians adopted the rose into their religious symbolism. The white rose often represented the Virgin Mary. The word "rosary" originally meant a rose garden but evolved to mean a series of prayers. Medieval cathedrals often used rose imagery in their rose windows: circular windows with petal-like panels radiating from the

Above: A yellow centifolia rose

Right: The entrance to the Heritage Rose Garden

center. Christian monasteries continued to cultivate the rose in their gardens for medicine, perfume, and communal wine.[6]

During the European age of exploration, trade between western Europe and the Far East expanded. In addition to silks and spices, living plants were traded. It is uncertain exactly when China roses made their way to Europe, but two China roses, 'Parson's Pink China' and 'Slater's Crimson China', were growing in England by 1792. It was the import of China tea roses that began the development of modern roses. Native European roses were large and beautiful but only flowered once during a growing season. China roses were smaller but flowered repeatedly from spring until frost.

Cultivation of roses flourished under the empire of Napoleon I of France. The Empress Josephine was

Left: 'Elina', a hybrid tea rose, can range in color from a creamy yellow to vanilla depending on soil conditions.

Below: Famous rose hybridizer Dr. Griffith Buck developed exceptionally hardy roses to survive midwestern winters at his laboratory in Iowa.

the daughter of a planter from the Caribbean island of Martinique and developed a keen interest in flowers, especially roses. She collected rose species from all over the world to grow in her rose garden at Malmaison in France. With her husband conquering the world, it was easy to gain access to all kinds of rose specimens. She commissioned the artist Pierre-Joseph Redoute to paint her roses. Redoute's watercolor collection *Les Roses* is a classic work. Empress Josephine also commissioned botanist Claude-Antoine Thory to catalog her collection. For the first time, serious work to botanically classify the different species of roses was accomplished.

So respected was Empress Josephine's work that French ships captured by the British with rose specimens aboard were allowed to continue to France. When France was conquered by the British

Above: Pink gallica rose 'Complicata'

Right: A species rose, Rosa sericea pteracantha, *is as old as the dinosaurs. It can be recognized by its huge red thorns.*

Left: 'Baroness Rothchild', a hybrid perpetual rose

Below: 'Champrey's Pink Cluster', a climbing Noisette rose

in 1815, the gardens at Malmaison were protected by British troops. Unfortunately, without royal patronage, the gardens at Malmaison soon fell into disrepair, but the larger mission had been accomplished. A French rose industry continued to develop and propagate new roses for an expanding market of French landowners.[7]

European breeders in the mid-nineteenth century introduced the Portland, Noisette, tea, and hybrid perpetual roses. They were the first attempts to create repeat-blooming roses with the color range and flower size of old European roses. In Asia, Chinese breeders were perfecting the China roses.

By 1900, breeders concentrated on flower shape, color variety, cold hardiness, and disease resistance to develop the hybrid tea, polyantha, floribunda, grandiflora, miniature, and shrub roses that we know today.[8]

Rose Test Garden 4

Elizabeth Park has been testing roses since 1912. Its first affiliation was with the American Rose Society which requested that a rose test garden be added to its original Rose Garden design by Theodore Wirth. Elizabeth Park became the first rose test garden site in the United States. In 1936, another rose test garden was added to the Elizabeth Park Rose Gardens at the request of the American Rose Society. Their convention was held in Hartford in 1937.

Over the years, there have been several suspensions of Elizabeth Park's rose test program. Each time, Elizabeth Park risked losing its prestige as a premier rose garden. The American Rose Society and now the All-American Rose Selections give participating parks access to new rose varieties and up-to-date practices in disease control and rose culture.

The first suspension was in 1933, during the height of the Great Depression, when funding around the country was in a crisis. The second suspension was when Everett A. Piester was promoted to park superintendent in 1954. Hartford did not hire a horticulturist to replace him. No one else in the city's employ was certified as a

Opposite Page: 'Queen Elizabeth' is one of the most popular and reliable grandiflora roses grown today.

Below: Rose arches

Above: The rose garden at dusk

Right: 'Love's Promise' is a velvety red hybrid tea rose.

rosarian and rose test judge to oversee the rose testing. It was then that Charles Meli, future park superintendent, studied to become a certified rose test judge so the program could resume at the park.[1] The third suspension was in 1977 when a fiscal crisis almost prompted the entire Rose Garden to be plowed under.

HISTORY OF THE ROSE TEST PROGRAM

Before official rose test gardens, the development of roses was an unorganized affair. Rose plants were first brought to America by European colonists. A rose industry developed, and many plants were offered for sale by various American nurseries. From the Civil War era to the early twentieth century, thousands of rose varieties were offered. There were often duplicates or those so closely resembling each other it was impossible to recognize one variety from another. There were no standards for breeding. Many roses were of inferior quality and were not honestly presented to the public. Breeders also had little incentive to spend their

'Francois Michelon' is an original hybrid perpetual rose planting.

'Sunsprite', a floribunda rose, is as sunny as its name.

51

time and money on developing new rose varieties when they had no patent protection for their work.

The American Rose Society was founded in 1892 to guide rose enthusiasts. It relied on rose test gardens to provide honest and accurate information about new varieties. Still, little work was done to hybridize new varieties of roses until the United States Plant Patent Act of 1930. Finally, protection was provided to plant breeders. Inventors were now able to control their new creations for seventeen years and collect a royalty payment. Now there was real compensation for the years of work involved in developing new rose varieties. Rose patents poured into the United States Patent Office, but unfortunately many were of inferior quality. The rose-growing public continued to be fooled, and at a higher price.

Above: 'Party Time', a hybrid tea rose, is reminiscent of a frilly party dress.

Right: 'Daybreaker', a floribunda rose, has the unusual color combination of yellow and pink.

It became clear to all those sincerely interested in roses, including the American Rose Society, that an organization had to be created to oversee the testing of new rose varieties to honestly assess the merits of each new plant and report these findings to the rose-buying public. Two groups started in 1937 in the east and west and combined in 1938 to become the All-American Rose Selections organization. In 1938, the All-American Rose trial garden system was created.[2]

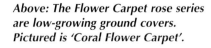

Above: The Flower Carpet rose series are low-growing ground covers. Pictured is 'Coral Flower Carpet'.

Right: 'Dainty Bess' is a modern single-petaled rose.

The American Rose Society is now a national organization with over 24,000 members dedicated to the enjoyment, enhancement and promotion of America's Floral Emblem. The ARS has evolved over the years into a nonprofit organization for home gardeners who enjoy growing roses and want to expand their knowledge of rose culture. The ARS also guides its members in the exhibition of their roses in competition with other rose lovers. The American Rose Society has developed standards and guidelines for these competitions.[3]

The All-American Rose Selections currently oversees the development of new rose varieties. The main goal of AARS is to develop roses that can be grown anywhere in the United States where roses are normally grown with top performance. Anyone who buys a rose with the AARS seal of approval can rely on a rose of excellent quality.

Above: 'Lady of the Dawn' is a hybrid tea rose.

Right: An inviting park bench beckons a visitor to sit and admire the roses.

Above: The 'Dorothy Perkins' rose arches are one hundred years old.

Left: A rose-lined fence surrounds the rose garden on all sides.

HOW A ROSE BECOMES AN AARS WINNER

The AARS has a relationship with rose hybridizers who develop roses to the standards of the AARS in exchange for publicity and acclaim to help in the sale of their new roses. Once a new rose is developed by a rose hybridizer, test plants are sent to twenty sites throughout the United States. These roses are then tested for two years under all soil and climate conditions that exist in the United States. Test gardens for the AARS must be maintained by their specifications to resemble a normal garden by an ordinary good home gardener. The roses are then judged by an officially trained AARS judge assigned to each rose test garden. Most AARS judges are college professors or horticulturists in charge of large public gardens who take their judging appointments very seriously. Judges score roses based upon the AARS Scoring System that rates rose characteristics such as color, fragrance, stem, vigor, habit, hardiness, disease resistance, foliage, flower production, bud and flower form, and overall value. An average of fifty new rose hybrids are entered into the AARS rose trials each year. Only five percent of the roses entered into the trials over the history of the AARS have received high enough scores to be considered AARS winners. Sometimes only one rose receives the AARS award each year, and in 1951 no rose met their requirements.

Above: The white eyes in shrub rose 'Heart 'N' Soul' stand out when grouped together.

Right: 'Fame', a hybrid tea rose, has a distinctive creamy center.

*'George Washington' is another
original hybrid perpetual
rose planting.*

*Above: 'Olympiad', a hybrid tea
rose, was developed to be the
official rose of the 1984 Summer
Olympics in Los Angeles.*

*Right: A red climber growing on
a fence*

Once AARS winners are selected, the AARS Publicity Committee promotes the new rose varieties. The most commonly used media to disseminate information to the rose-growing public are newspapers, magazines, and gardening publications. The AARS knows that once they send their press releases to these media organizations, the awards are accepted without question. Soon the news is passed on to other forms of media including the Internet. New roses are presented with a background of their history and developers, along with descriptions of their most outstanding characteristics. Rose nurseries eagerly promote these new rose varieties, since their sales exceed other rose varieties each year as home gardeners are looking for new roses of high quality.[4]

Above: 'Top Notch', a floribunda rose, is considered tops in color.

Right: 'Bride's Dream', a hybrid tea rose, is popular in wedding bouquets.

'Duet', a hybrid tea rose, is a popular pink variety.

The All-American Rose trial garden system has proven to benefit all involved. Hybridizers have an organization to test and promote their roses, nurseries have roses of high quality to sell to satisfied customers, public gardens have visitors eager to view upcoming new varieties, and gardeners can be assured of roses that will perform well in their gardens.

'Tiffany' blossoms are smaller than those of the average hybrid tea rose.

Annual, Perennial, and Rock Gardens
of Elizabeth Park

The Rose Garden is the most famous feature of Elizabeth Park, but it also contains other gardens with rich histories. One garden that has passed into memory is the famous Sunken Garden. Theodore Wirth created a formal garden with turfed steps, knotted shrubbery and exotic plants in 1905. It can now only be viewed on many of the postcards of yesteryear. Located behind the Pond Estate House facing Prospect Avenue, only rhododendrons, flowering trees, and spring flowers now grace the informal space where the Sunken Garden and its graceful home once stood.

*Opposite Page: Yellow coneflower (**Rudbeckia**)*

Below: The Sunken Garden was highly cultivated with exotic plants.
(Connecticut State Library)

ANNUAL GARDEN

Many people, including myself, never considered tulips to be annual flowers. At Elizabeth Park, eleven thousand tulip bulbs are planted anew each year. This ensures a spectacular display every spring. When the flowers fade, the bulbs are sold to the public. Thousands of visitors flock to the Annual Garden every spring to view the tulips and return to buy the bulbs at bargain prices.

Next, the garden beds are planted with annual flowers started by seed in the greenhouses. All winter and early spring, visitors can tour the

Above Left: A bed of red celosia dazzles the eye.

Above: Eleven thousand tulip bulbs are planted in the Annual Garden every year.
(Photo Courtesy of Diana Lyn Cote)

Left: Yellow marigolds contrast nicely with blue ageratum.

greenhouses and view the seedlings that will eventually make their way to the Annual Garden.

Another aspect of the Annual Garden are the dahlia flowerbeds maintained by the Connecticut Dahlia Society. These beds are located next to the historic greenhouses. The culmination of their hard work is exhibited during their annual Dahlia Show.

The Herb Garden is another part of the Annual Garden. It is situated near the greenhouses. This sunken, square plot contains plants and walkways surrounding a central statuary in the typical design of herb gardens.

Above: Sunflowers tower over zinnias in the Annual Garden.

Left: Every year this standard form of lantana, a native of South America, is brought out into the Annual Garden from the shelter of the greenhouse.

Left: Creeping thyme covers the bed around the herb statue.

Below: Dahlias are grown in special raised beds.

PERENNIAL GARDEN

There has always been a Perennial Garden at Elizabeth Park. Unfortunately, by the 1980s, the garden was a shadow of its former grandeur. Improvements began with the construction of an open wooden pavilion to provide a focal point for small gatherings and weddings. Funds were provided by the Larus Foundation and the Hartford Foundation of Public Giving.

The Friends of Elizabeth Park hired perennial garden expert Frederick McGourty of Norfolk, Connecticut to restore the garden area in 1987. With funds from the Hartford Foundation for Public Giving, McGourty

The Herb Garden is designed in the traditional style of walkways with a center statuary.

65

Above: A bed of iris (Iris siberica) is blooming early.

Right: Red poppies (Papaver orientale) stand out in the early summer.

widened and redesigned the existing beds. He also enclosed the area with a dwarf Japanese yew hedge *(Taxus browni)*, allowing for openings from the Rose Garden, Lilac Hedge, Rock Garden, and Annual Garden. Eight perennial beds are arranged around the Pavilion. Two sets of flowers in cool colors (blue, pink, and lavender) and two sets of flowers in warm colors (yellow, orange, and red) are planted directly opposite each other. More than sixteen hundred new plants were added. Only a few yucca and daylily plants were saved from the original garden.

Each spring, Marc Tonan, a horticultural consultant who helped McGourty plant the new Perennial Garden, opens the beds by adding new plants, dividing old plants, fertilizing, and mulching. This eases the maintenance of the perennial beds by the City of Hartford gardeners for the rest of the season.[1]

Above: The Perennial Garden has a border of Japanese yew with the Pavilion at the center.

Left: 'Basket of Gold' (Aurinia) has tiny yellow flowers that appear in early summer.

Hardy geranium 'Johnson's Blue' (Geraniaceae) makes a good ground cover.

Right: Crocosmia (Crocosmia masoniorum) provides interesting texture in a perennial border.

Left: Bright white Shasta daisies (Leucanthemum) stand out from the other flowers.

Right: Phlox (Polemoniaceae) *can hug the ground or tower above the garden, as with this red specimen.*

Left: Yarrow (Achillea filipendulina) *blooms in many colors, but yellow is most prevalent.*

Peonies (Paeonia) *originated in China and Japan. They are one of the most popular perennial flowers grown in the garden.*

69

Above: Bees are especially attracted to purple onion (Allium giganteum).

Below: A weeping larch tree forms the entrance to the Rock Garden.

ROCK GARDEN

The first Rock Garden in Elizabeth Park began in 1914. The Rock Garden is a European idea originating in Austria. They were called Alpine Gardens and designed to imitate a mountain environment and its plants. Rock gardens became very popular in the United States in the 1920s and 1930s. Ironically, major influences for this type of garden came from England where the Kew Gardens still maintains its famous Rock Garden.

Unfortunately, like many other garden features in Elizabeth Park during the recession prone 1970s, the Rock Garden had fallen into serious disrepair. In 1981, the Friends of Elizabeth Park contracted horticultural consultant Julian Eddy to redesign and replant the Rock Garden. The beds were rearranged and a red stone wall was added. A rejuvenation of Eddy's original design was accomplished by Marc Tonan in

1994. Tonan was able to use many of the existing beds, trees and shrubs. Low-maintenance ground covers, perennials, and annuals, all well suited to a rock garden environment, were added. Pathways were widened to facilitate accessibility for the handicapped. A rededication ceremony in memory of Julian Eddy took place on June 27, 1995. The Rock Garden has become a favorite spot where visitors can rest in the shade and take in the beauty of Elizabeth Park.[2]

Above: The Rock Garden is a favorite resting spot for visitors.

Right: Hostas enjoy the shade of a dawn redwood tree.

The Trees of
6
Elizabeth Park

Charles M. Pond was a lover of exotic trees and shrubs. When he willed his estate to the City of Hartford, Elizabeth Park Superintendent Theodore Wirth kept many of his trees in the park design. Wirth also added trees that are now a century old. Laurel Pond, the manmade pond that exists today, was ringed with spruce, hemlock, and pine trees. Many of these plantings remain. The estate was a working farm and had orchards of fruit trees. Wirth removed these trees because they did not fit into the design of a pastoral park.

Connecticut is a leader in forestry. By 1830 much of the countryside had been cleared for farming and agriculture, with less than prosperous results. People began to leave Connecticut and move west, abandoning their rocky and hilly farmsteads in search of better and plentiful land, now that goods could be easily transported by rail back to the eastern population centers. The landscape of Connecticut began changing back to the dense forested cover that exists today.

The year 1896 saw the development of the Connecticut Forestry Association, which was later to become the Connecticut Forest and Park Association

Opposite Page: The shagbark hickory (Carya ovata), *a native of the United States, gets its name from its distinctive bark.*

Below: The nuts of the shagbark hickory (Carya ovata) *are edible.*

(CFPA). The main objective of the association was to develop public appreciation of the value of forests and of the urgent need for preserving and using them properly. Connecticut was the first state in the country to have a state forester and state forest lands. Additional laws were passed at this time that also provided for town tree wardens and the care and protection of shade trees.

The Yale School of Forestry, the oldest in the nation, was founded in the year 1900. Connecticut became the first state in the country to introduce scientific forestry. Yale continues to be the leading school of forestry in the country.

Interest in land conservation and forestry was also developing at the national level. In 1891 a federal law was passed that allowed for the creation of forest reserves across the United States. These reserves eventually became our National Forests. A Connecticut native, Gifford Pinchott, was

Above: The katsura tree **(Cercidiphyllum japonica)** *is a native of Japan and China, where it has grown to one hundred thirty feet.*

Right: The katsura tree **(Cercidiphyllum japonica),** *a native of Japan and China, has beautiful heart-shaped leaves.*

Above: Elizabeth Park's Tree Trail rings the park.

Above Right: A dogwood (Cornus) in spring bloom.

Right: Seed pods of the American sweetgum (Liquidamber styraciflua)

instrumental in this process and became the chief forester of the United States in 1905.[1]

There are forty-three notable trees on the Elizabeth Park Tree Trail. A pamphlet guides the visitor to all the distinguished trees in the park. The loop is an easy flat walk less than a mile long.

The oldest trees are the many oaks that grace the park. The Connecticut Botanical Society has designated several trees as State Champions, the largest of their species in Connecticut. The mono maple and golden larch in Elizabeth Park are such trees.[2]

Above: Black birch (Betula lenta), a native of the United States, is named for its distinctive dark bark.

Right: Mono maple (Acer mono), a native of Asia, is a State Champion at sixty feet tall.

Left: Rhododendron shrubs line the south side of Elizabeth Park. Pictured is Rhododendron loderi.

Below Left: This weeping blue spruce (Picea pungens 'Glauca Pendula') is a State Champion at thirty feet tall.

Below: The pine cone of the weeping blue spruce (Picea pungens 'Glauca Pendula').

Elizabeth Park
Features

When Charles M. Pond left his estate to the City of Hartford for a park, he left a working farm with its various farm buildings, orchards, and sloping meadows. The work done to create the level graded lawns and drives that we see today was no simple feat. Elizabeth Park has many beautiful manmade features that have solved landscaping problems and enhanced its beauty.

ELIZABETH PARK GROUNDS

Work on Elizabeth Park began in 1897 when Theodore Wirth hired the Olmsted firm to design the grounds. Although Olmsted himself was retired, his sons carried on his philosophies. Working together, the Olmsted firm and Mr. Wirth added new drives and pathways, drained the meadows, built bridges and created the pond. Drainage of the west section of the park was especially difficult. Two miles of drainage pipe was installed to spill into the pond. The overflow from the pond created a stream that meandered into the woods. A rustic boulder bridge was built over the stream, and a rough wooden bridge was built over a narrow neck of the pond. A rustic gate was also erected at the south park entrance at Walbridge Street.[1]

Opposite Page: A garden walkway in Elizabeth Park

Below: After Laurel Pond was created, a rustic wooden bridge was built over the pond's narrow neck.
(CONNECTICUT STATE LIBRARY)

Above: Sunrise Overlook was an open expanse of meadows with a direct view of Hartford. Now the city skyline can only be seen peeking over the century-high trees.

Right: Sheep were kept at Elizabeth Park to trim the lawns. Lambs, born every spring, were a favorite visitor attraction.
(CONNECTICUT STATE LIBRARY)

Formal overlooks were established at each end of the park: Sunrise and Sunset. One hundred years ago, these overlooks had an open and commanding view of the surrounding countryside. Sunrise Overlook was an open expanse of meadows leading to a much smaller Hartford. Only the capitol dome was visible rising from the open meadows. Now the city skyline is crowded with skyscrapers peeking over century-high park trees. Sunrise Overlook was renovated in the 1980s with garden beds and stone walls for closer appreciation since the

A rustic wooden gate was erected at the end of Walbridge Street, the south entrance to Elizabeth Park. (Connecticut State Library)

commanding view is now obscured by trees, high wires, and city streets and homes. Sunset Overlook, once taking in an impressive view of the Talcott Mountain valley, is now completely obscured by the suburban homes and streets of West Hartford.

The south entrance today, without a gate

81

The Boulder Bridge was built to span the manmade stream that took the runoff from Laurel Pond.
(CONNECTICUT STATE LIBRARY)

It was decided to employ a flock of sheep to keep the lawns trimmed. This was considered more pastoral, and thus more in keeping with the philosophies of the American Park Movement. The sheep were a favorite visitor attraction. A sheepfold was kept in the park for their shelter. This was later turned into the first skate house for winter visitors.[2]

In 1901, the drives were widened and electric cars were first admitted to the park. The cars created a constant stream of traffic and brought a daily crowd of visitors. By the following year, there were complaints that the "automobilists ran their machines too fast through the park showing off their machines rather than truly enjoying the park." A rule of six miles per hour was enforced.[3]

The Boulder Bridge covered in snow captures the pastoral look by its designers.

The Boulder Bridge has endured since its original construction. It is now surrounded by tall trees and shrubs. After seven years, the rustic bridge over the pond had deteriorated badly. A decision was made to create a more permanent stone bridge in 1905. This bridge remains today.[4]

Above: The Stone Bridge was built in 1905 to replace the deteriorated rustic bridge.
(Connecticut State Library)

Below: The Stone Bridge looks much the same after a century.

ELIZABETH PARK BUILDINGS

There were many farm buildings on the Pond Estate. All these barns were assembled in one area, and the Lord & Burnham Company was hired to build the greenhouses in 1898. The greenhouses today are the original buildings and are in the process of being restored. Often referred to as the "Nursery" in park reports, Elizabeth Park greenhouses provide flowers for all municipal buildings in the city.

The lower part of the Pond Estate House was renovated to accept park visitors. The original furniture was removed and wicker furniture was

Above: The historic greenhouses are currently under restoration.

Below Right: The Visitor Center once housed the gardener foreman and his family.

added. There was also a library.[5] In 1900, a refreshment counter was opened by Mr. Joseph Besse in the Pond Estate House.[6] The second floor housed the park super-intendent and his family. Theodore Wirth's first son was born in the house.[7] Unfortunately, the Pond Estate House was demolished in 1956.

The Elizabeth Park Visitor Center that houses the offices of the Friends of Elizabeth Park is a structure older than the park itself. It was moved to the park in 1897 to house the Elizabeth Park foreman and his family. Tom Queeno was the last gardener foreman to live in the house with his family in the 1970s. Like a lighthouse keeper, the foreman was a constant protective presence in the park. But, privacy was non-existent. People would enter their home as if it were a public building and use their picnic table for lunching!

The Pond House was built in 1959, replacing the razed Pond Estate House as a place for park visitors to seek shelter from the elements and take refreshment. It currently houses the Pond House Café, a fine-dining restaurant. There is also a large meeting room that can be rented for group functions. The spring and fall flower shows take place in the Pond House every year.

Above Left: The current Pond House now features the Pond House Café, a fine-dining restaurant.

Above: Gardeners repot pansies started in the Nursery for use around Hartford.
(HARTFORD PUBLIC LIBRARY)

The most recent structure is the Elizabeth Park Pavilion built in the 1980s. It provides a resting place for garden visitors and a backdrop for wedding pictures. In early summer, it is flowing with purple and white clematis: a spectacular sight!

The Pavilion at the center of the Perennial Garden is beautiful when its clematis is in full bloom.

Activities 8 *in*

Elizabeth Park

ELIZABETH PARK RECREATIONAL AREAS

By the early 1900s, Hartford's grand park experiment hit a snag. The design of the parks as natural country settings, becoming very dark at night, was attracting negative human activity. In 1902 lighting was constructed in Elizabeth Park to discourage vagrants, drunks, and prostitutes. Many of the Hartford parks lost their tree and shrub boundaries to become more visible to policemen from the street. Since Elizabeth Park was considered the "garden park," it retained more of its plantings.

Opposite Page: People enjoy sitting under a stand of Black Tupelo (Nyssa Sylvatica) which are named after the water nymph Nyssa, due to their high water requirements.

Below: The first playground equipment was a merry-go-round in 1902.
(CONNECTICUT STATE LIBRARY)

Elizabeth Park received a merry-go-round from the Hartford Machine Screw Company in 1902. This gift was the beginning of providing recreational family-oriented activities for park visitors. The park now has two playground areas.

One favorite park activity, once enjoyed especially by children but no longer allowed, is the feeding of waterfowl at the pond. Since Canadian Geese began wintering over in Connecticut twenty years ago, they have become a serious pest by fouling

One of two playgrounds in Elizabeth Park is a modern playscape.

ponds across the state. Elizabeth Park has not been spared this problem. A large family of geese can be seen living by the pond. The ducks must compete for space and food with their larger relatives.

Ice-skating is another dim memory for park visitors. Connecticut has enjoyed mild winters for the past few decades. Skating on thin ice is dangerous and was finally discouraged completely. However, cold, long, New England winters seem to be making a comeback. Hopefully, ice-skating at Elizabeth Park will begin again.

Many visitors enjoy the pleasant surroundings to take a leisurely walk, jog, or bicycle on the many trails provided in the park. Sunbathers sprawl on lawns in the summer. Many walkers bring their dogs. Even in the dead of winter, tracks can be seen in the snow as visitors take in the quiet solitude of the park.

Ice-skaters enjoy a winter's day in 1953, before the construction of the present-day Pond House.
(HARTFORD PUBLIC LIBRARY)

Elizabeth Park provides many recreational fields. They are situated away from the gardens and often out of view. Many tourists, who come from far away to visit the gardens, do not even know of the existence of these recreational features, but they are used extensively by local visitors. Baseball fields and tennis courts are found on the east end of the

Picnicking under the cooling shade of tall trees is very popular on summer weekends.

Bicycling is a popular activity.

89

Above: The tennis courts of Elizabeth Park

Above Right: The Thistle Lawn Bowling Association has maintained its field since 1913.

park. A football field, available during the start of its popularity, is no longer seen at the park. One sport of yesteryear that is still played at Elizabeth Park is lawn bowling. The Thistle Lawn Bowling Association began in 1913. It almost died out a few years ago but now has forty-five members and is growing. Lawn bowling is a genteel game with strict etiquette rules and a dress code during tournaments. It is especially challenging because the ball is flat on one side and does not always roll as expected!

The 2003 winners of the Connecticut Rose Show are festooned with ribbons.

The Letterboxing Club has even designated Elizabeth Park for one of its Treasure Hunt activities. Letterboxing is an intriguing pastime and hobby that uses navigational skills in a quest to find a box in various locations.

CELEBRATIONS IN ELIZABETH PARK

There have been picnics in the park since its beginning. Many families gather for reunions, graduations, and other celebrations. Banners can be seen strung from trees to hail family members and announce the event. The picnic area is situated away from the flower gardens under the cooling shade of century-old trees so that inviting aromas do not compete with the scent of the flowers!

Taking wedding photos among the beautiful gardens of Elizabeth Park is another very popular activity. From early spring into late autumn, wedding parties can be seen every weekend lining up in front of the blooms of the moment. There is always a spot of color in Elizabeth Park. Many couples choose to perform their wedding ceremony at the park. The rustic summer cottage and the Pavilion are the most favorite spots for wedding ceremonies.

Above: Elsa Nieves prepares to walk down the rose arches to meet her bridegroom Elvin Cotto.

Left: Carol Malicki and Peter Antonelli during their first moments as a married couple in Elizabeth Park.

ARTISTS OF ELIZABETH PARK

Elizabeth Park has been the inspiration for many artists. Most famous is poet Wallace Stevens. He walked through Elizabeth Park every day on his way to work and often stopped to reflect and write. Several of his poems are about Elizabeth Park.

Artist Diana Lyn Cote is strongly associated with the park due to her longtime love of painting it. Her unique style is based on a twist of impressionism. Other artists who paint scenes from the park are Cheryl Davis, another impressionist artist, and Stephen Fournier, who specializes in watercolors.

Thousands of photographers come to Elizabeth Park with their cameras. Many photographers share their experiences by publishing their photographs on websites.

Vacancy in the Park
> March…someone has walked
> across the snow,
> Someone looking for he knows
> not what…
> It is like the feeling of a man
> Come back to see a certain
> house
> The four winds blow through
> the rustic arbor
> Under the mattress of vines.
>   ***Wallace Stevens***

> Well, how 'bout a red rose
> Or maybe a rainbow
> How 'bout we linger 'til dark here
> in Elizabeth Park
> What have we here: isn't it clear
> I'm singing a red rose
> You're painting a rainbow
> We're making these memories of
> Elizabeth Park & true love…
>   ***Excerpt from "Elizabeth Park"***
>   ***by Rex Fowler***

There are always concerts at the park. Music can be heard almost every weekend. A permanent grandstand for musicians can be seen near the Rose Garden. One musician, Rex Fowler, has featured a song named "Elizabeth Park" on his new CD *Gettysburg*.

In all seasons, the park is filled with people from near and far. Some come for quiet reflection, while others are actively engaged. People are reading, eating, admiring the flowers, listening to music, playing tennis, hitting a baseball, running, biking, pushing strollers, taking pictures, or simply walking the grounds. Footsteps can be seen in the snow in the middle of winter. It is a place where people from all walks of life can come together and appreciate a beautiful space in the middle of a bustling city. The hopes and dreams of the American Park Movement live on at Elizabeth Park.

Above: A mother and child enjoy the flowers.

Below: The Connecticut Rose Society offers a rose pruning demonstration free to the public.

Notes

Chapter 1:

1. Alexopoulos, John, *The Nineteenth Century Parks of Hartford: A Legacy to the Nation*, (Hartford, Conn.: Architecture Conservancy, 1983).

Chapter 2:

1. Cranz, Galen, "Changing Roles of Urban Parks: From Pleasure Garden to Open Space," *The San Francisco Planning and Urban Research Association*, January 2, 2003. <http://www.spur.org/urbparks.html>.

2. Alexopoulos, John, *The Nineteenth Century Parks of Hartford: A Legacy to the Nation*, (Hartford, Conn.: Architecture Conservancy, 1983).

3. "100 Years of Hartford Parks," *Hartford Courant*, November 6, 1994.

4. Hollister, George H., *The Rain of Parks*, Articles 1–6, circa 1936.

5. "Charles M. Pond Dead," *Hartford Courant*, September 9, 1894.

6. Dean, Clarence, "Battle of Pond House Stirs Echoes of Lush Past: Park Named for Banker's Wife," *Hartford Times*, June 27, 1953.

7. "Charles M. Pond Dead," *Hartford Courant*, September 9, 1894.

8. Dean, Clarence, "Battle of Pond House Stirs Echoes of Lush Past: Park Named for Banker's Wife," *Hartford Times*, June 27, 1953.

9. "The Pond Will," *Hartford Courant*, February 24, 1896.

10. Groark, Virginia, "The Pond House Stew," *Hartford Courant*, November 18, 2001.

11. "Pond Will Broken," *Hartford Courant*, March 16, 1896.

12. "Verdict Set Aside," *Hartford Courant*, March 30, 1896.

13. "Burr Fund Case Recalls Will Battle over Elizabeth Park," *Hartford Times*, August 22, 1949.

14. Dustin, Dan, "Theodore Wirth," *Texas A&M University Department of Recreation, Park, & Tourism Sciences*, January 6, 2003. <www.rpts.tamu.edu/Pugsley/Wirth%20.htm>.

15. Baldwin, Peter C. *Domesticating the Street: The Reform of Public Space in Hartford, 1850-1930*, (Columbus, Ohio: Ohio State University Press, 1999).

16. "Piester Seen Slated as City Parks Head," *Hartford Times*, April 9, 1954.

17. "Hollister A/B," *UCONN Residential Life*, July 30, 2003, <www.reslife.uconn.edu/reshalls/West/west.cfm>.

18. "City Would Raze Old Pond House," *Hartford Times*, April 2, 1952.

19. "Pond House Repairs to Cost $16,814," *Hartford Times*, May 26, 1952.

20. Dean, Clarence, "Battle of Pond House Stirs Echoes of Lush Past: Park Named for Banker's Wife" *Hartford Times*, June 27, 1953.

21. "Historic Pond House to Get Face-Lifting," *Hartford Times*, July 28, 1953.

22. "E. A. Piester, 82, Ex-Rose Garden Curator Dies," *Hartford Courant*, November 23, 1973.

23. "Work Date Set on Pond House," *Hartford Times*, August 24, 1954.

24. "Mayor Kinsella Accuses City Manager of Misuse of Funds," *Hartford Courant*, December 9, 1958.

25. "Kinsella Claims City Charter Violated," *Hartford Courant*, December 10, 1958.

26. "Official Charges Filed by Mayor," *Hartford Courant*, December 12, 1958.

27. "Sharpe Responds to Council," *Hartford Courant*, December 14, 1958.

28. "No Architect Contract Signed, Council Is Told," *Hartford Courant*, December 30, 1958.

29. "Hearing Set for City Manager," *Hartford Courant*, December 23, 1958.

30. "Never Again," *Hartford Courant*, January 7, 1959.

31. "Council Votes 6–3 to Censure Sharpe," *Hartford Courant*, January 15, 1959.

32. "Everett J. Pyle Named Deputy Park Director," *Hartford Times*, December 13, 1954.

33. "Long-Time Nature Lover," *Hartford Times*, June 21, 1970.

34. "Director of Parks Appointed," *Hartford Courant*, July 16, 1969.

35. "Parks' Fates Hang on Suburbs," *Hartford Courant*, May 21, 1975.

36. "Council Unit Backs Rose Garden Fees," *Hartford Courant*, October 7, 1975.

37. "City Loses Money on Park Fee," *Hartford Courant*, October 22, 1976.

38. "City Wipes Out Fee for Garden," *Hartford Courant*, May 10, 1977.

39. "End Asked to Costly Rose Fee," *Hartford Courant*, May 3, 1977.

40. "West Hartford May Aid in Elizabeth Park Upkeep," *Hartford Courant*, July 23, 1977.

41. Sandberg, Jon, "$10,000 Gift Pledged to Park," *Hartford Courant*, June 11, 1978.

42. Sandberg, Jon, "Elizabeth Park Funds Proposal Receiving Favorable Reaction," *Hartford Courant*, June 12, 1978.

43. Sandberg, Jon, "Two-Town Six-Member Committee on Elizabeth Park Proposed by Ludgin," *Hartford Courant*, June 26, 1978.

44. Giacomo, Carol, "City has $1.5 Million Plan to Redesign Elizabeth Park," *Hartford Courant*, September 12, 1978.

45. Sandberg, Jon, "Elizabeth Park Application Endorsed," *Hartford Courant*, November 29, 1978.

46. "Elizabeth Park Funds Rejected," *Hartford Courant*, January 23, 1979.

47. "Elizabeth Park Rose Garden to Bloom with New Rose Bushes," *Hartford Courant*, April 13, 1978.

48. "100 Years of Hartford Parks," *Hartford Courant*, November 6, 1994.

49. Neyer, Constance, "Rose Garden Wins National Acclaim," *Hartford Courant*, June 20, 1991.

50. Groark, Virginia, "The Pond House Stew," *Hartford Courant*, November 18, 2001.

51. "Judge Stirs Pond House Dispute," *Hartford Courant*, August 19, 2002.

Chapter 3:

1. Wirth, Theodore. *New Elizabeth Park Rose Garden Proposal*. July 28, 1903.

2. Deitz, Paula. "Design Notebook," *The New York Times*. June 24, 1982.

3. Wirth, Theodore. *New Elizabeth Park Rose Garden Proposal*. July 28, 1903.

4. "Park Department Seeking Fund to Fight Jap Beetle," *Hartford Times*. August 15, 1936.

5. "City Starts Waging War on Beetles," *Hartford Times*. August 26, 1936.

6. Edinger, Philip. *Roses*. Menlo Park, California: Sunset Publishers, 1998.

7. "History of Roses." *Urban Programs Resource Network University of Illinois*. January 15, 2003. <http://www.urbanext.uiuc.edu/roses/history.html>.

8. Edinger, Philip. *Roses*. Menlo Park, California: Sunset Publishers, 1998.

Chapter 4:

1. "City Gives Up Elizabeth Park Rose Testing." *Hartford Times*. June 4, 1955.

2. Rose, George E., ed. *Fifty Years of Dedication: Creating Excellence in the Rose, America's National Flower*. Omaha, Nebr.: Interstate Printing, 1988.

3. American Rose Society Homepage. *American Rose Society*. <http://www.ars.org>.

4. Rose, George E., ed. *Fifty Years of Dedication: Creating Excellence in the Rose, America's National Flower*. Omaha, Nebr.: Interstate Printing, 1988.

Chapter 5:

1. Wagner, Lina. "The Perennial Garden at Elizabeth Park." *The GreenThumbPrint*. Hartford, Conn.: Knox Parks Foundation. summer 1997.

2. Wagner, Lina. "A Garden That's Travelled Some Rocky Roads." *The GreenThumbPrint*. Hartford, Conn.: Knox Parks Foundation. summer 1997.

Chapter 6:

1. "History of Greenways: Recreational." *New England Greenway Vision Project*. <http://www.umass.edu/greenway/Ct/History/CT-HG-rec.html>.

2. *Trees of Elizabeth Park*. Hartford, Conn.: Friends of Elizabeth Park. summer 2003.

Chapter 7:

1. *Thirty-Ninth Annual Report of the Board of Park Commissioners of the City of Hartford*. Hartford, Conn.: Board of Park Commissioners of the City of Hartford, April 30, 1898.

2. *Fortieth Annual Report of the Board of Park Commissioners of the City of Hartford*. Hartford, Conn.: Board of Park Commissioners of the City of Hartford, April 30, 1903.

3. *Forty-Third Annual Report of the Board of Park Commissioners of the City of Hartford*. Hartford, Conn.: Board of Park Commissioners of the City of Hartford, April 30, 1903.

4. *Forty-Fifth Annual Report of the Board of Park Commissioners of the City of Hartford*. Hartford, Conn.: Board of Park Commissioners of the City of Hartford, April 30, 1905.

5. *Thirty-Eighth Annual Report of the Board of Park Commissioners of the City of Hartford*. Hartford, Conn.: Board of Park Commissioners of the City of Hartford, April 30, 1898.

6. *Forty-First Annual Report of the Board of Park Commissioners of the City of Hartford*. Hartford, Conn.: Board of Park Commissioners of the City of Hartford, April 30, 1900.

7. Neyer, Constance. "Tribute Paid to Rose Garden Designer," *Hartford Courant*, June 1, 1993.

Sources

Alicia Cornelio, Author of *Elizabeth Park: A Century of Beauty*
For additional copies of the book: *www.epcentury.com*

William Shepard, Photographer of *Elizabeth Park: A Century of Beauty*
For additional pictures from the book: *wmshprd@msn.com*

Connecticut Rose Society
1555 Asylum Avenue
West Hartford, CT 06117
www.ctrose.org

Diana Lyn Cote, Artist
www.dianalyncote.com

Friends of Elizabeth Park
1555 Asylum Avenue
West Hartford, CT 06117
www.elizabethpark.org

Pond House Café
1555 Asylum Avenue
West Hartford, CT 06117
www.pondhousecafe.com

Rex Fowler, Musician/Composer
Gettysburg CD
www.aztectwostep.com

About the Photographer

William Shepard is a full-time professional ophthalmic photographer. In addition, he offers freelance portrait, wedding, and commercial photography. He enjoys immersing himself in projects that call for different expressions of creativity. He found this project especially pleasurable; strolling through the fragrant paths of roses, trees and flora, learning the history of the park, and meeting the wonderful people associated with it. He used a vintage Rolleiflex camera, a newer Hasselblad camera, and a Canon camera, in an attempt to capture the beauty of a park that can only really be appreciated by being there.